A Diary of Emotions

Gloria Uwamahirwe

Presentation by *BookLeaf Publishing*

Web: www.bookleafpub.com

E-mail: info@bookleafpub.com

ISBN: 9789395969062

First edition 2023

DEDICATION

I am so grateful for all the fantastic people in my life. I have been blessed with friends and family who look out for me. This book, deals with some heavy topics. It is dedicated to everyone struggling to see the light at the end of the tunnel. One of my great friends once told me, "It gets better." I pray it gets better for you 

ACKNOWLEDGEMENT

I am so thankful to BookLeaf publishing for providing this opportunity. It is a dream come true. It's been one of my goals to publish something, and I can't believe that I have the chance to do this now.

Flytrap

I felt like a fly stuck behind a window whose
owner had refused to open,
Torturing me with the beautiful view of the
freedom I so desperately needed.
My mind was like darkness at noon.
It was a funeral and a wedding,
death felt so real,
yet no one mourned.
What once were rosy petals had turned into
hellebore flowers in their deepest purple; one
could mistake them for black.
My face felt numb,
My heart had been taken over by frostbite,
Reflections of the scars of the emotional wounds
he had caused.

An immigrant's cry.

Home,
Noun: a place where one lives permanently.

Where is home?
Does the constant moving render me homeless?
Does the search for safety and security make me any less?

I have no permanent home.
Never did, never will.
My home rejected me as its own,
Murdered, raped, and slew my own.
To remain patriotic or run to safety? I am torn.

My home is not permanent.
Has never been, will never be.
Refugee to the Citizen, I am free.
New culture, new life I get to live.
At least today, I can breathe.

My home will never be permanent.
Never was, nor is.
Continent to the continent I have been.
A whole new Process to begin.
Identify crisis, instability, and mental fragility.
Prize I pay for having no home.

insecurity

"You're not worthy!"
Words I've heard countless times,
From the girl in the mirror.
"You're not worthy!"
She said my waist should be perfect!
It's not slim enough,
I ate too much again.
"You're not worthy!"
Go to the gym, go on a diet!
I tried to keep this body happy, this facade,
But even I could not turn a blind eye to the dark lines
creeping up my waist,
The bumps and unsmooth skin on my thigh,
The growing pouch that won't fit in my pants anymore.
The girl in the mirror said, "if you were not so lazy, you
could fix this."
I tried, I really did,
"Not hard enough," she said
She is not happy with what she sees.
She tells me so.
What used to be my reflection, now I can't recognize
Maybe the girl in the Mirror is right...

sad.

The rivers are flowing nonstop.
The wells are overflowing.
Everything is drenched, but the feeling of dryness
overtakes.
An eerie quiet follows the current.

A rock is stuck at the near mouth,
It hurts the flow of water.
But the river is flowing,
The wells have overflowed.

The wind moves with the current.
The rock won't move.
The river roughly burbles against the eerie silence.
it's seamlessly flowing
The wells have overflowed.

She cries out in silence.
An invisible turmoil insid

Friends of the wind

Do your part
I'll do mine
Go your way
I'll find mine
We may be apart
We will reconnect again
Hopefully…

POV

You don't understand me,
I say something. You hear something else,
Always making it a big deal,
Always making it about you.
Try and see my point of view.

Will you listen for once?
Listen to what am telling you.
This is what your actions make me feel.
I don't want to hate you,
Understand my point of view.

Am always the first person you call when you need
something,
Am always the one you call when you want something,
But when I ask, you don't see the point.
You don't understand why I should.
Please understand my point of view.

When I get angry, I don't speak clearly,
My heart hurts each time we argue,
I guess some stuff gets lost in translation,
You always jump to a conclusion
Aggravating the situation,
Why don't you see my point of view?

Walk a mile in my shoes

anger

Don't make me the villain in my story.
Audacious in the way you viciously twist my
words.
In your presence, I am a measly sinner, and you
oh you are spotless.
Sitting in your self-appointed glory, you are
blameless.
Can't be touched, can't be humbled.
You are the villain.

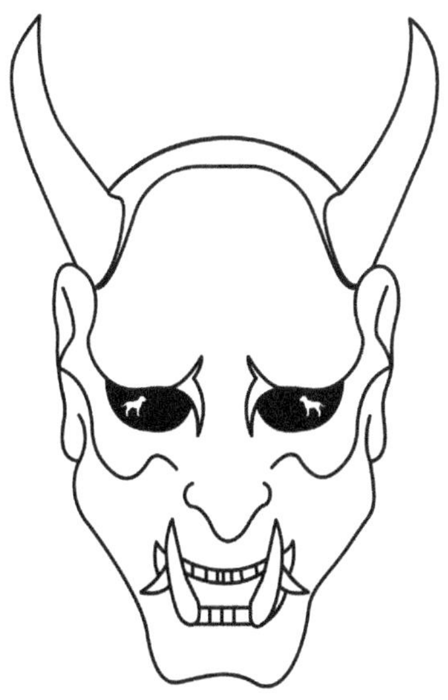

bluer

I wish to die a subtle death, nothing like this.
A peaceful moment to myself in complete bliss.
When I close my eyes, I see you
Reminiscing, I feel blue.
Time is supposed to heal all wounds.
But only time can tell when again, I will hear the tunes
That once brought a bloom to my aching body.

insomnia

Days start bleeding into the night
And nights into days.
Darkness surrounds as the mind runs 100 miles
per hour.
Unconscious thoughts, defeated thoughts,
bleeding thoughts brought by the heavy cross.
Thoughts of past mistakes consume the mind on
the what if's and the what nots.
It's exhausting.
The burden is heavy and overbearing.
Nights stretch long and overwhelming.
Ain't getting no sweet dreams tonight.

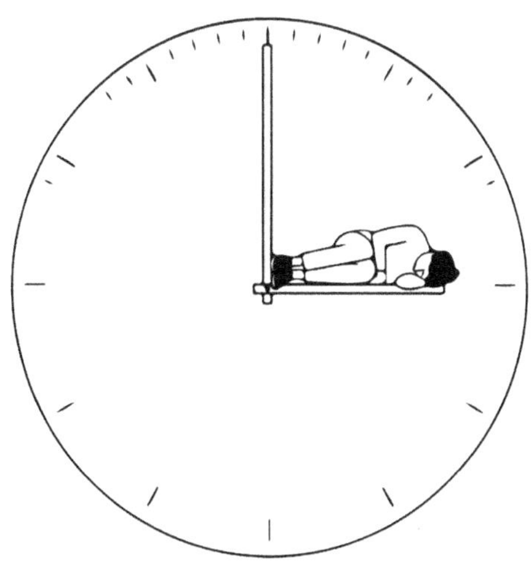

best lies.

Tell me all that I want to hear.
Even if it's not true.
The best kind of lies.
Coz that way I don't have to think of anything else.
That way I don't have to see the truth.

Happy.

I am happy.
Am I happy?
I should be happy,
Why am I not happy?

Smile.
If I smile, I'll be happy.
Yeah, that is it,
Smile more.
But what if I can't smile?

Fake it.
Can I fake happy?
I can't be that hard,
I'll fake happy.
How do I fake happy?

84

Look away so I can cry.
That's the only thing I ask you not to deny,
Thought my tears would have run dry,
I can't keep being the tough guy.
If I were to live without you, I would die also.

Look away so I can cry
Last time really felt like goodbye,
I don't want you to see the hurt in my heart
Amplified by the thought that you gave yourself a
head-start,
It is not yet time to depart, love.

Look away so I can cry
So I can wallow in self-pity and fall apart.
I'll swallow my tears for a few more minutes,
Paste a smile on your face, and follow your lead.
But my heart is already in sorrow.
So please look away so I can cry.

Promisor

Your unkept promises
Had me accepting that you ain't shit.
Promised the whole world, but not a single box
checked
It's disrespectful at this point,
Don't get me wrong; I know you ain't perfect,
But don't act suspect when I bring up to the
subject of your unchecked behavior,
I have learned not to expect anything from you.

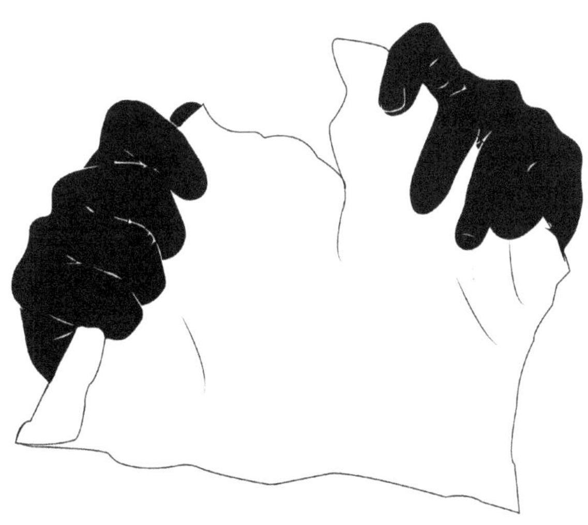

give n take

Take my mind and help me unwind.
Take my scars and give me perfect.
Take my thoughts and give me clarity.
Take my darkness and give me lighter days.
I can't do it all by myself.

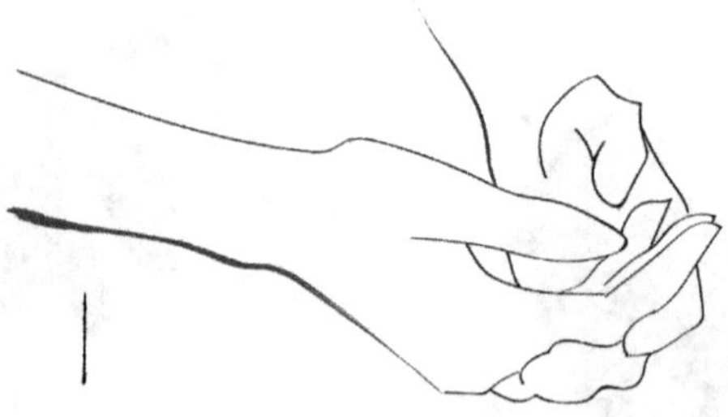

love.

In his eyes, I saw mine
In his heart, I saw mine

"If you'll have me."
I am yours

sunny days.

When the sun rise,
We can have it all.
We will dance barefoot on the dewy grass
We will feel the sun's rays on our skin,
We will have it all.
When the sun rise,
The darkness will be no more,
Gone will be the days stuck in bed,
the ones that felt never-ending.
The sun will rise.

A prayer

May the Almighty protect you from the invisible
monsters.
From the tortures that keep you up at night,
And the foux friends and imposters, the ones
who claim to be day oners.
From lonely nights and the midnight horrors.
May He give you peace of mind,
And be combined with softer smiles.
Provide you with real love that describes what it
is to live again.
Amen.

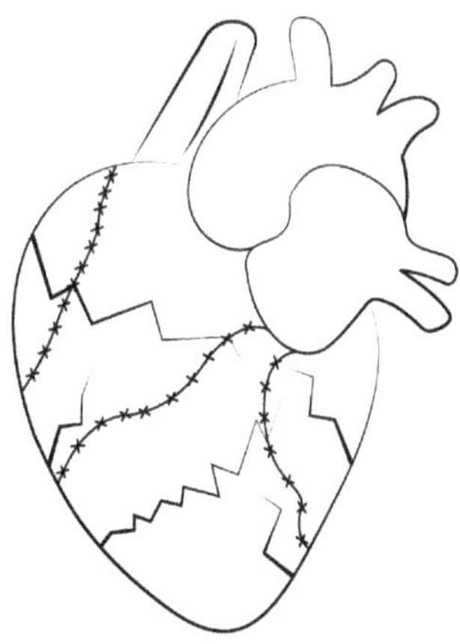

Lonely Fields

Big empty fields,
Stained with vibrant green.
They yearn for a purpose,
To grow, to be vibrant.
Those beautiful lonely fields,
Stained with a pale yellow
They long for company,
To have children play in them
To be colorful, to be loved.

freezing

I am cold.
On this hot summer day,
I am freezing cold.
A cold that consumes your insides,
Leave's nothing but Ice.
A cold that yearns for warmth.
You can't get this kind of warmth from physical heat,
You don't, I've tried.
This warmth warms the heart.
My heart is cold.

hopeful

I hope we get to look back and say, "we've come a long way."
Celebrate our journey,
our pain,
and every moment that almost had us.
That almost made us quit.
That almost won over us.
We will sit back
watching the sunset
with a drink in our hands
and reflect on how much we have grown.
How much we are happier,
We get to be happy now.
We will pleasantly sigh
as a satisfied smile sits on our face
Grateful that we persevered,
Because we won. We beat the demons.
We are alive.

thank you 🖤

I am thankful
For the 'how was your day.'
And the 'text me when you get home.'
For the prayers and the love you share.
Thank you for being there when I didn't deserve
you.

9 789339 596062